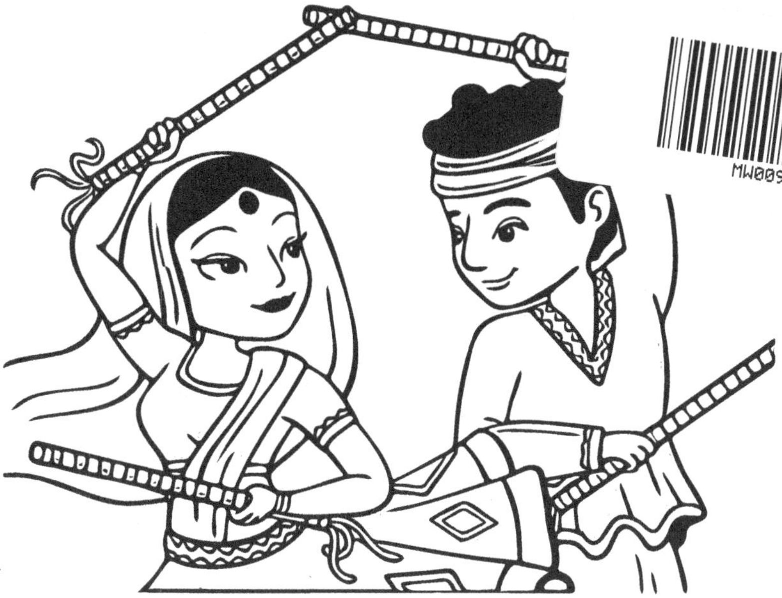

NAVRATRI COLORING BOOK FOR KIDS

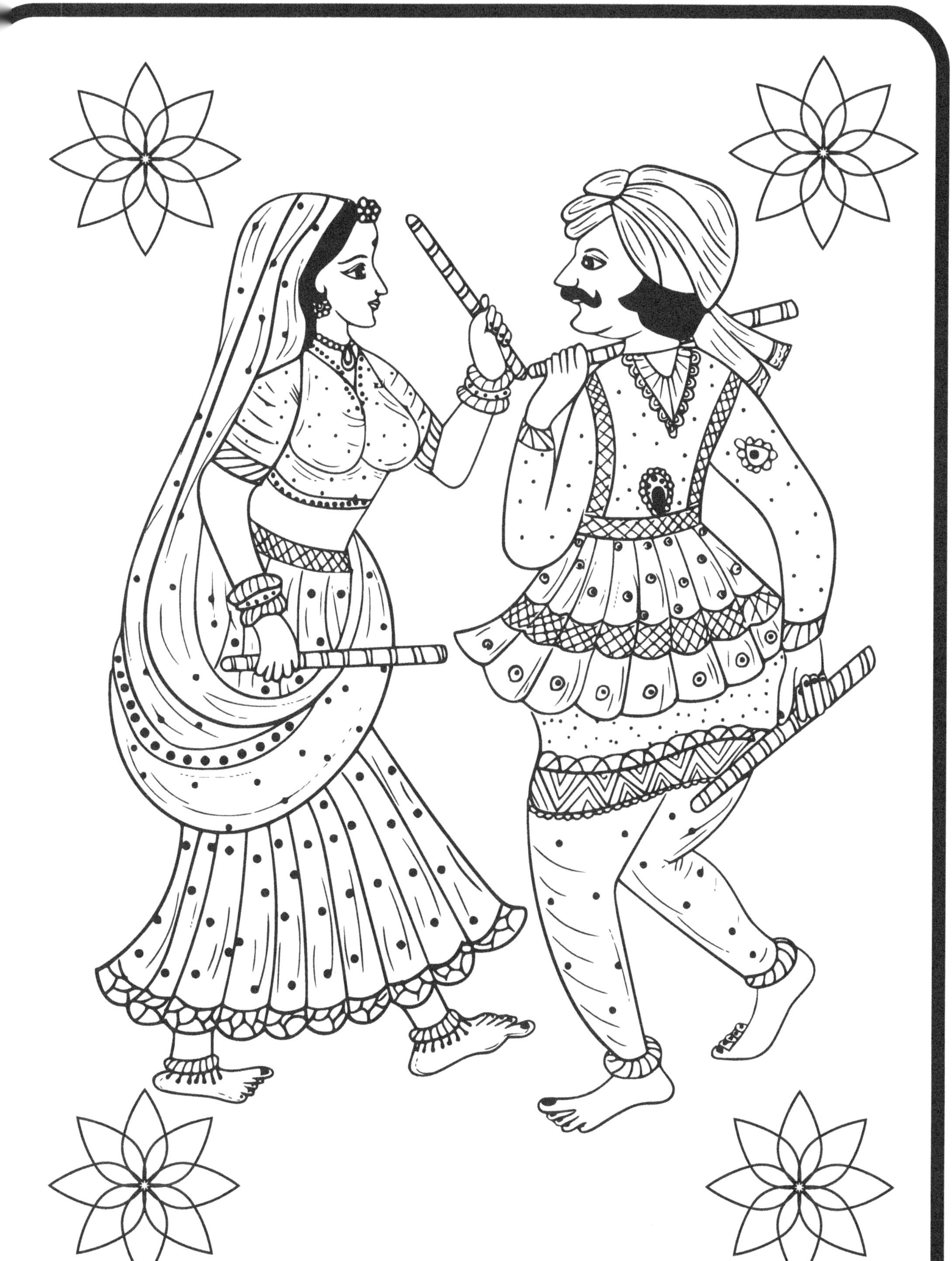

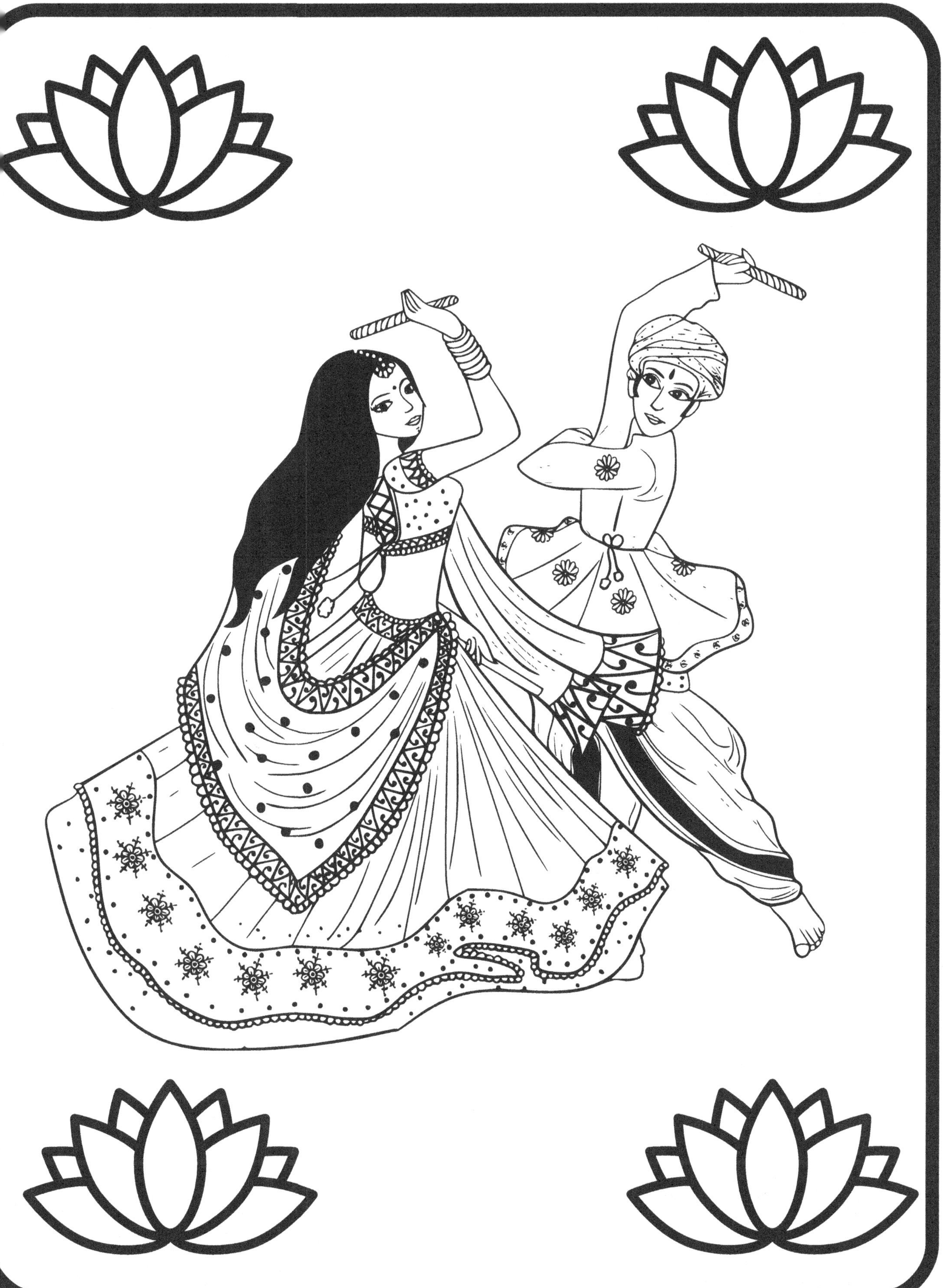

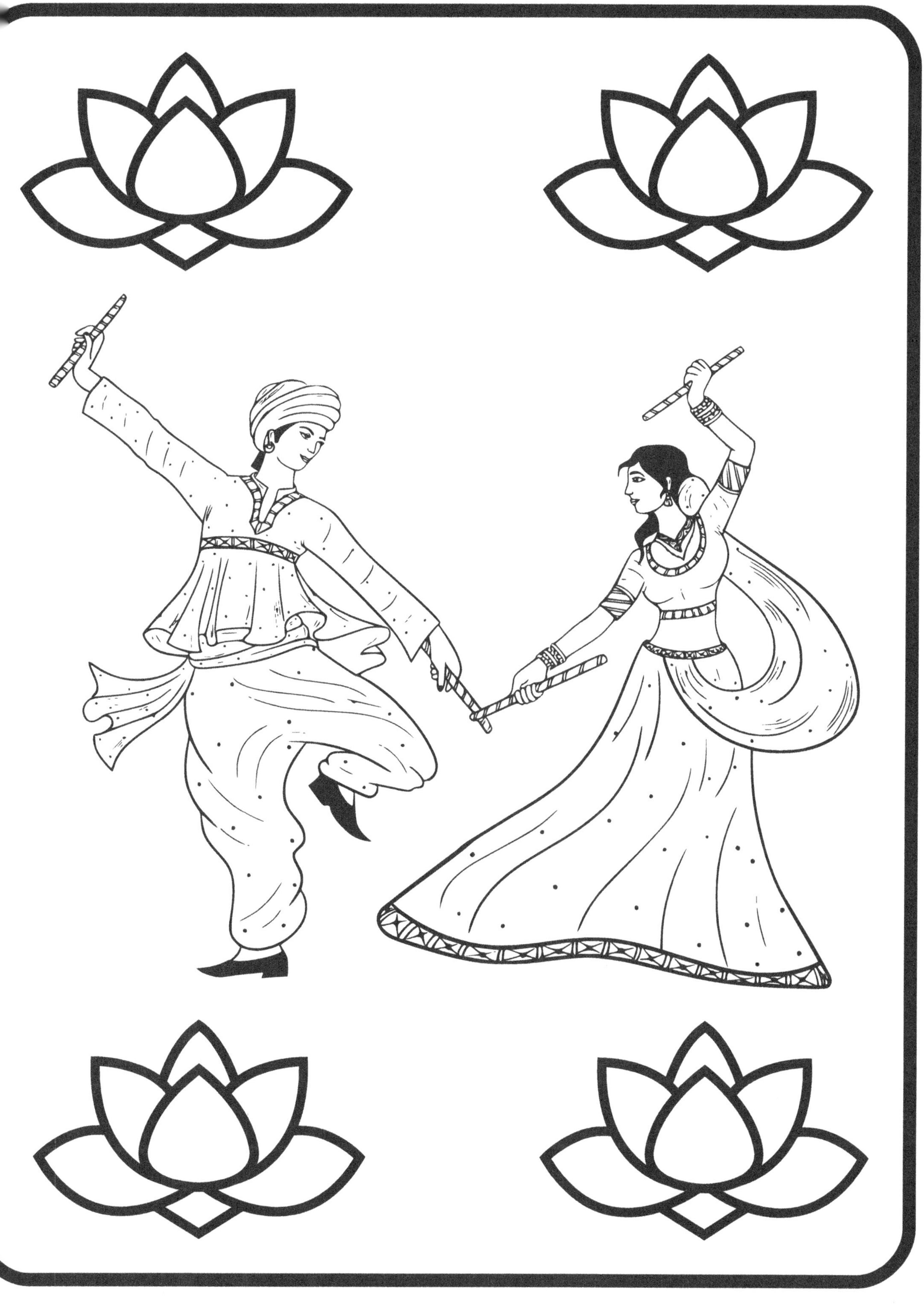

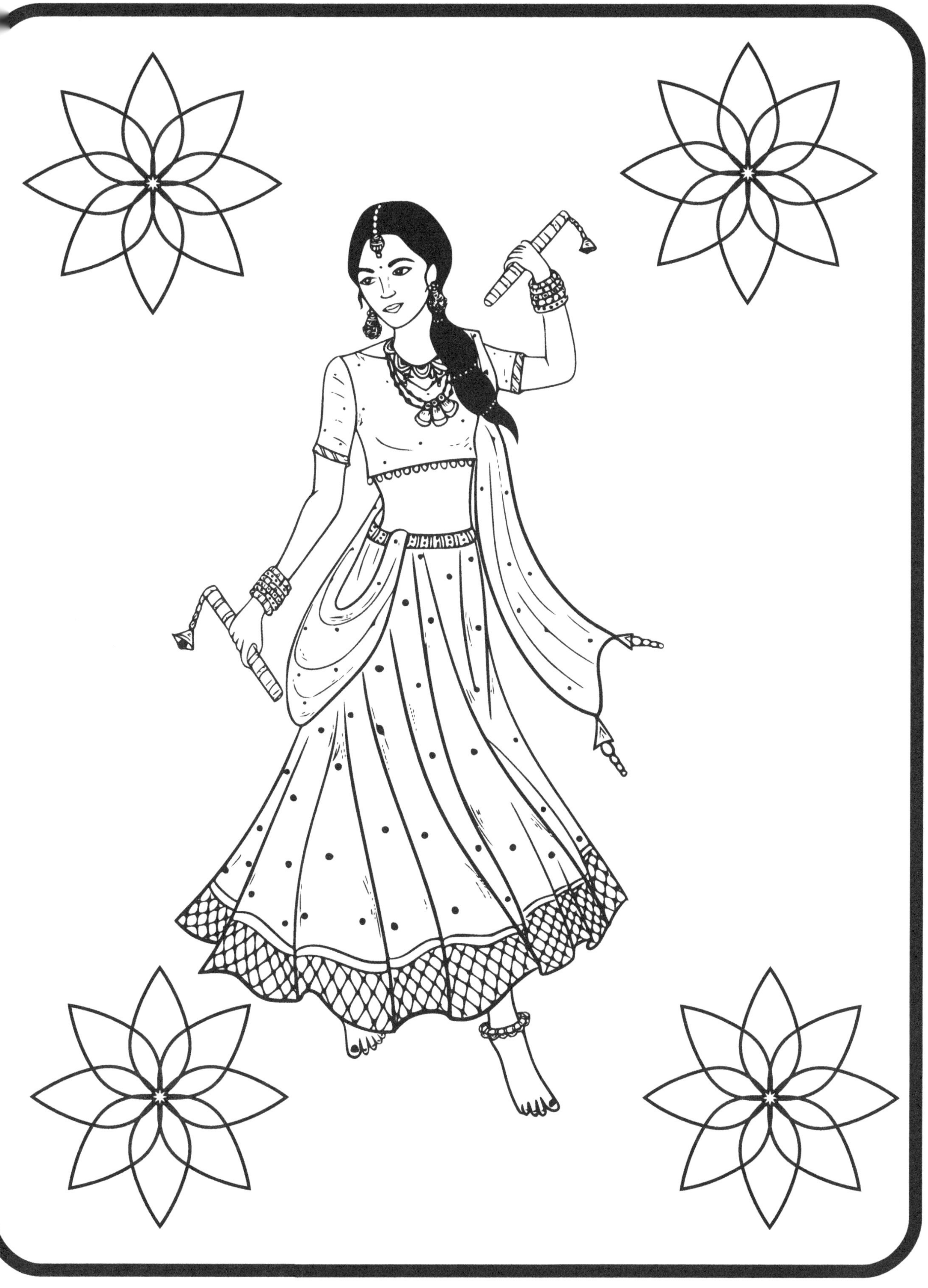

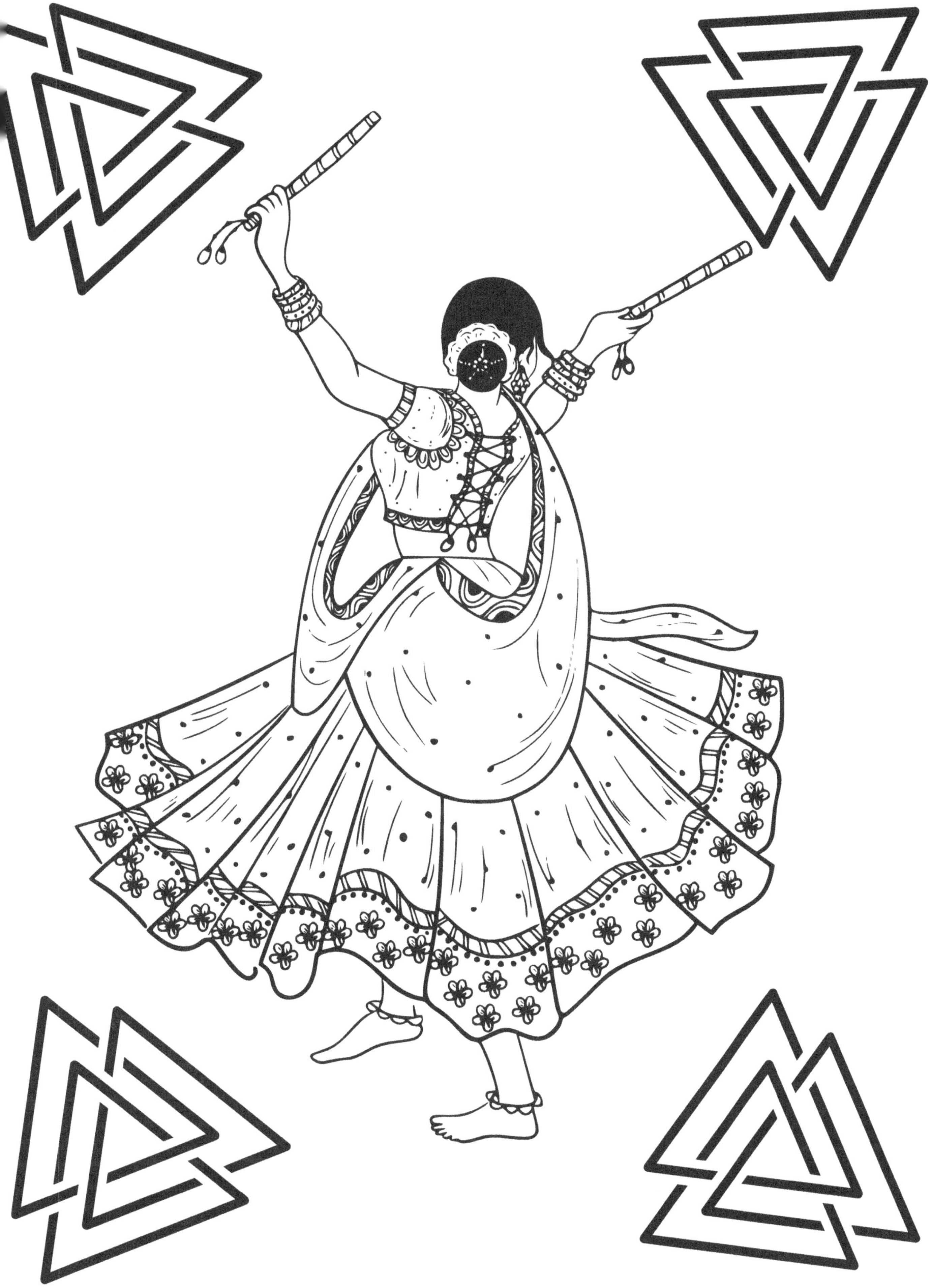

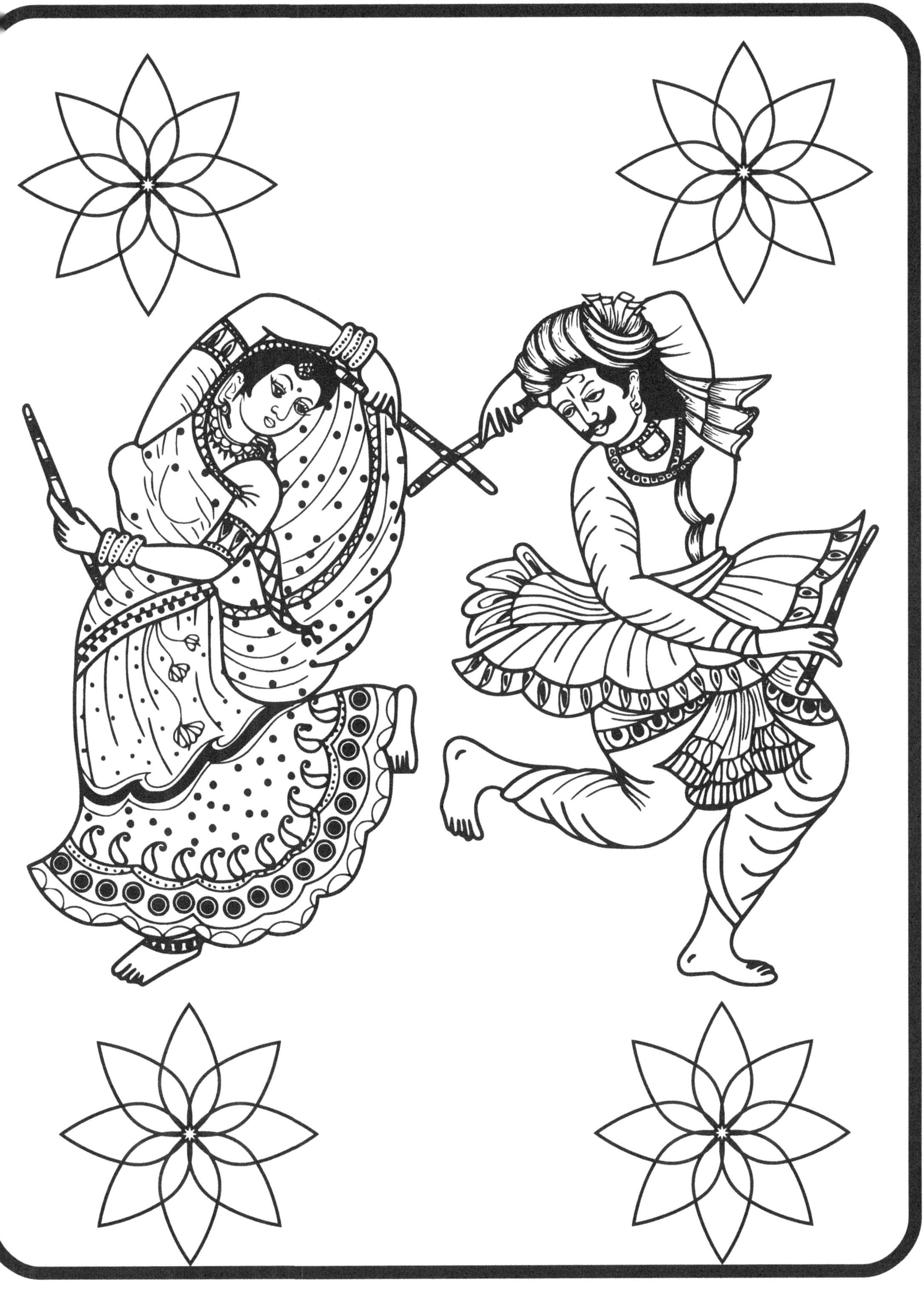

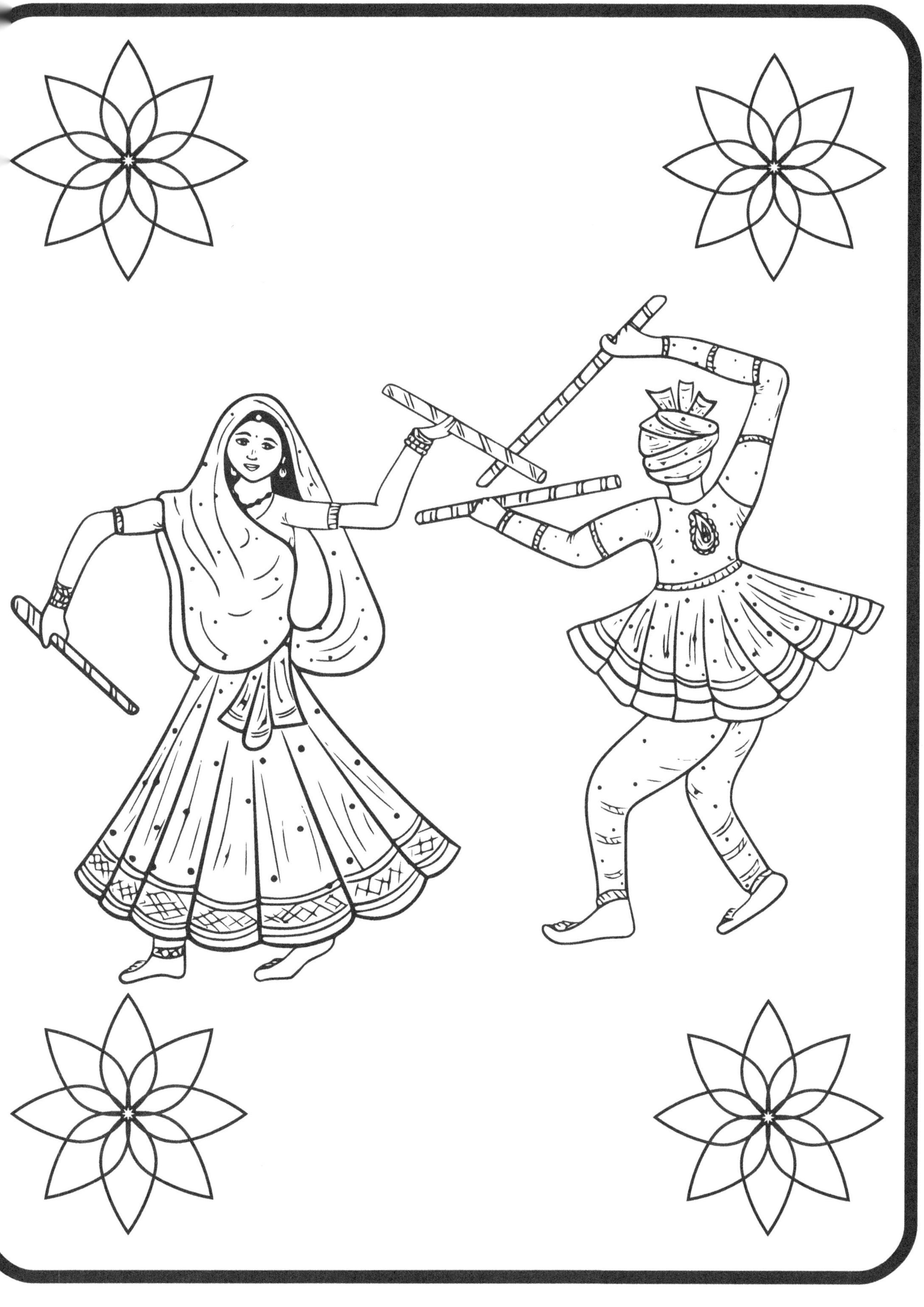

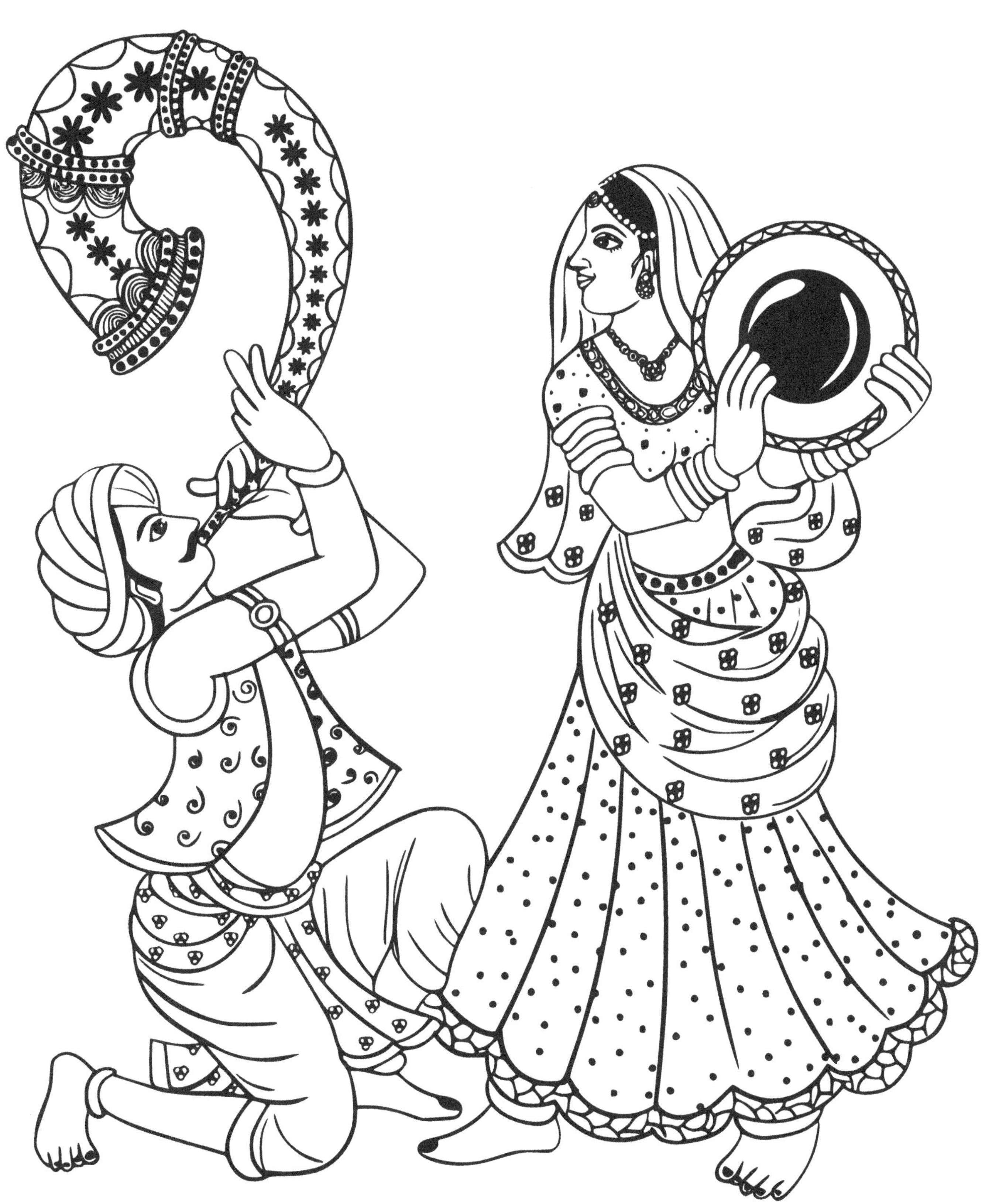

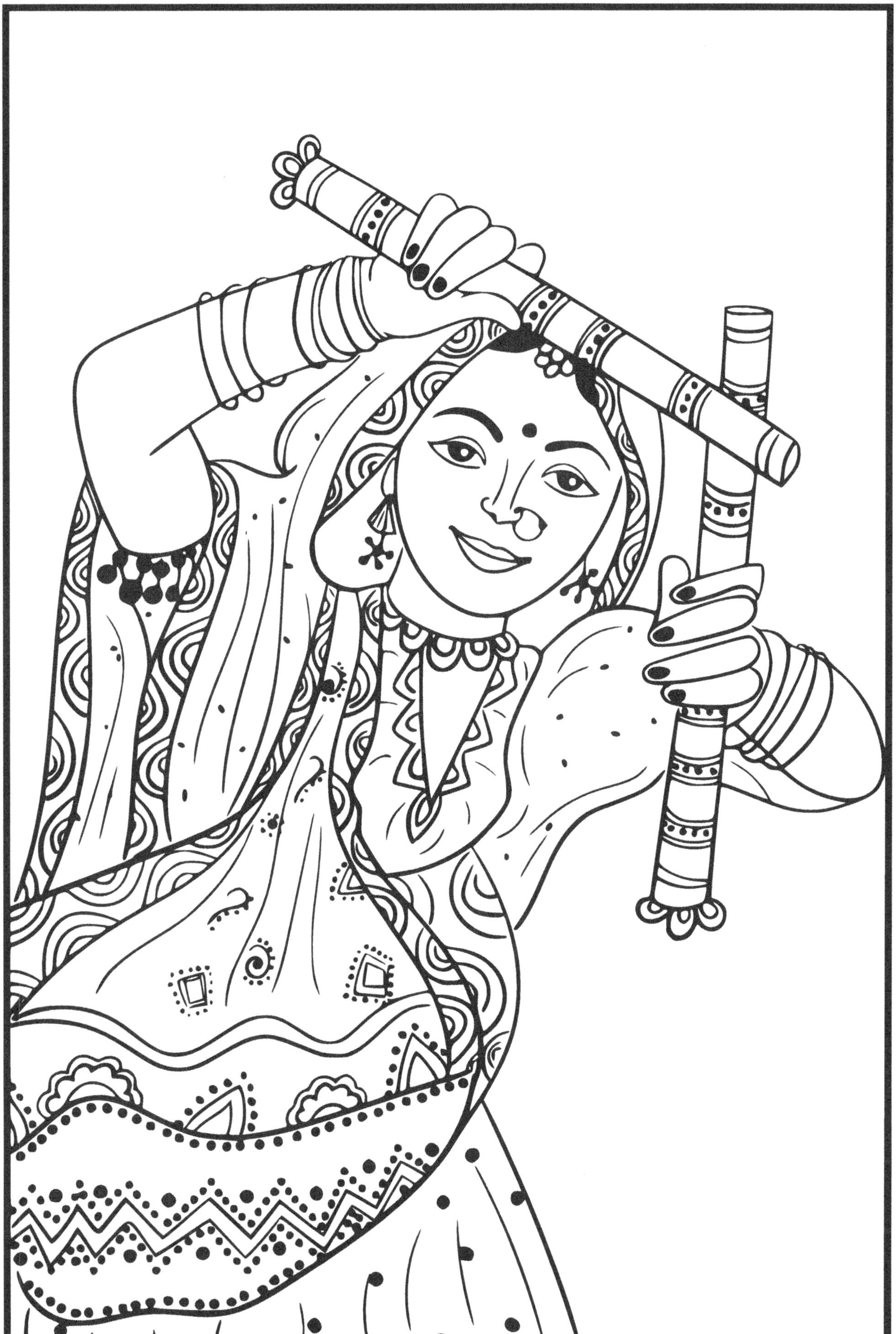

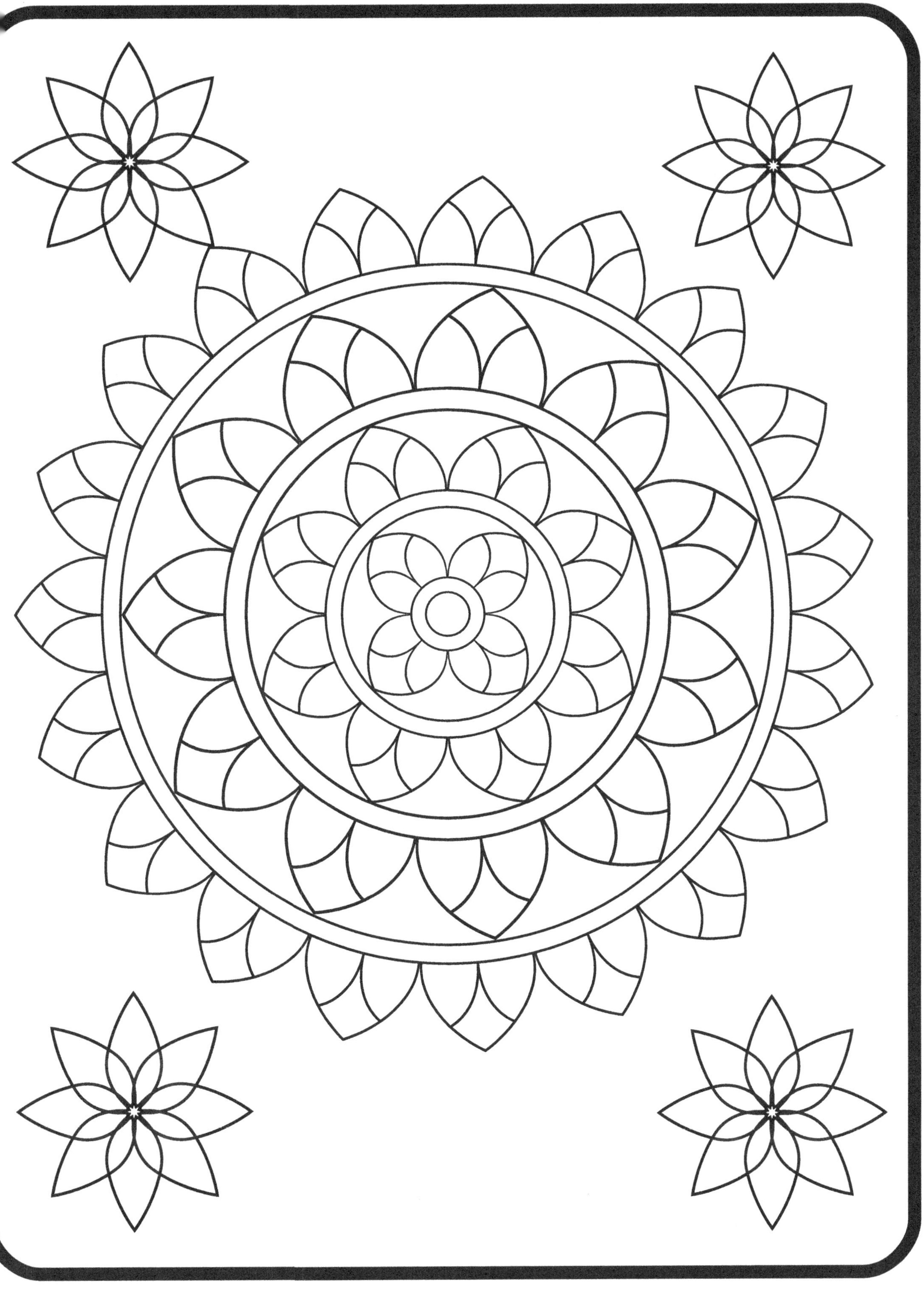

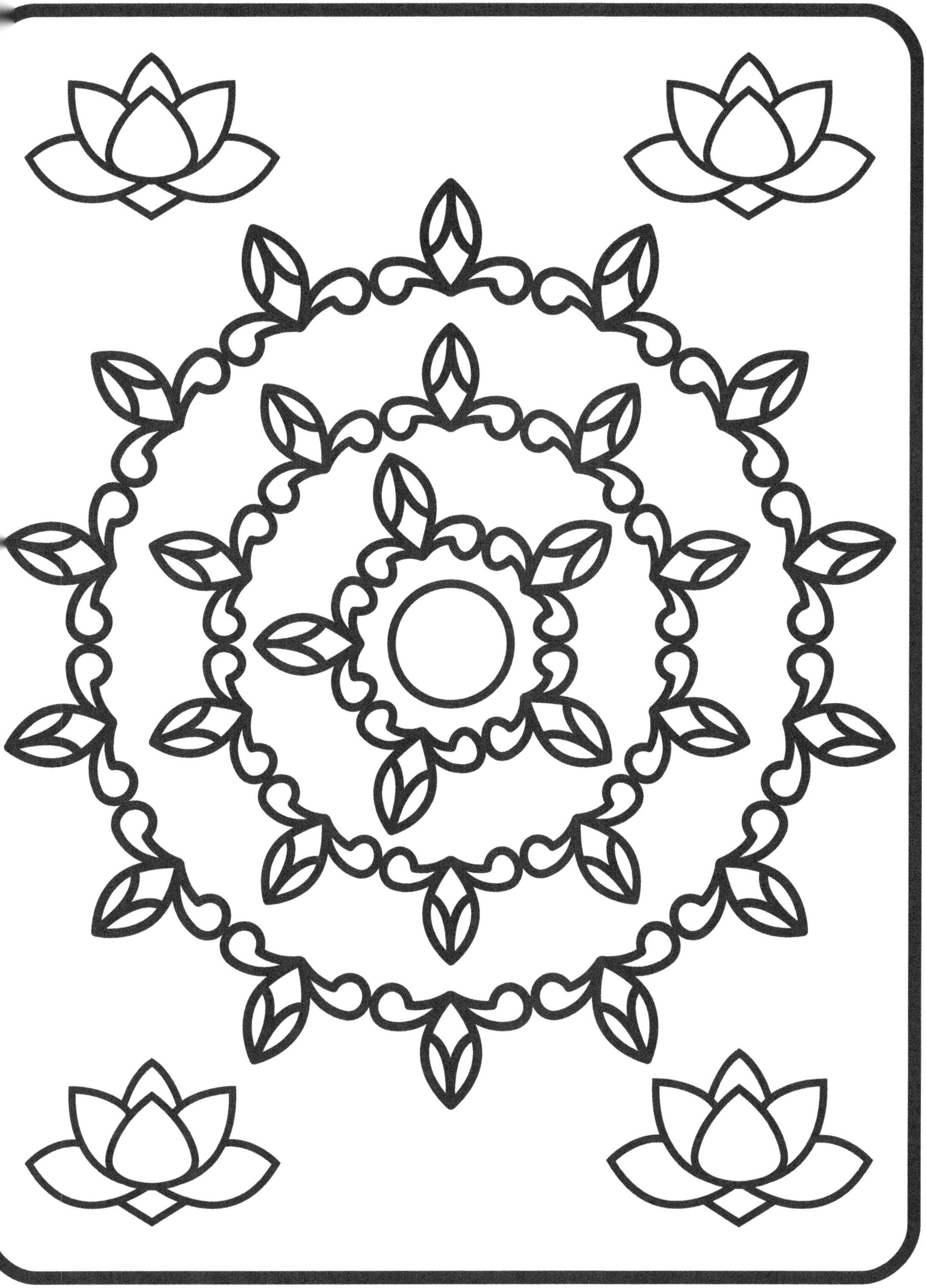

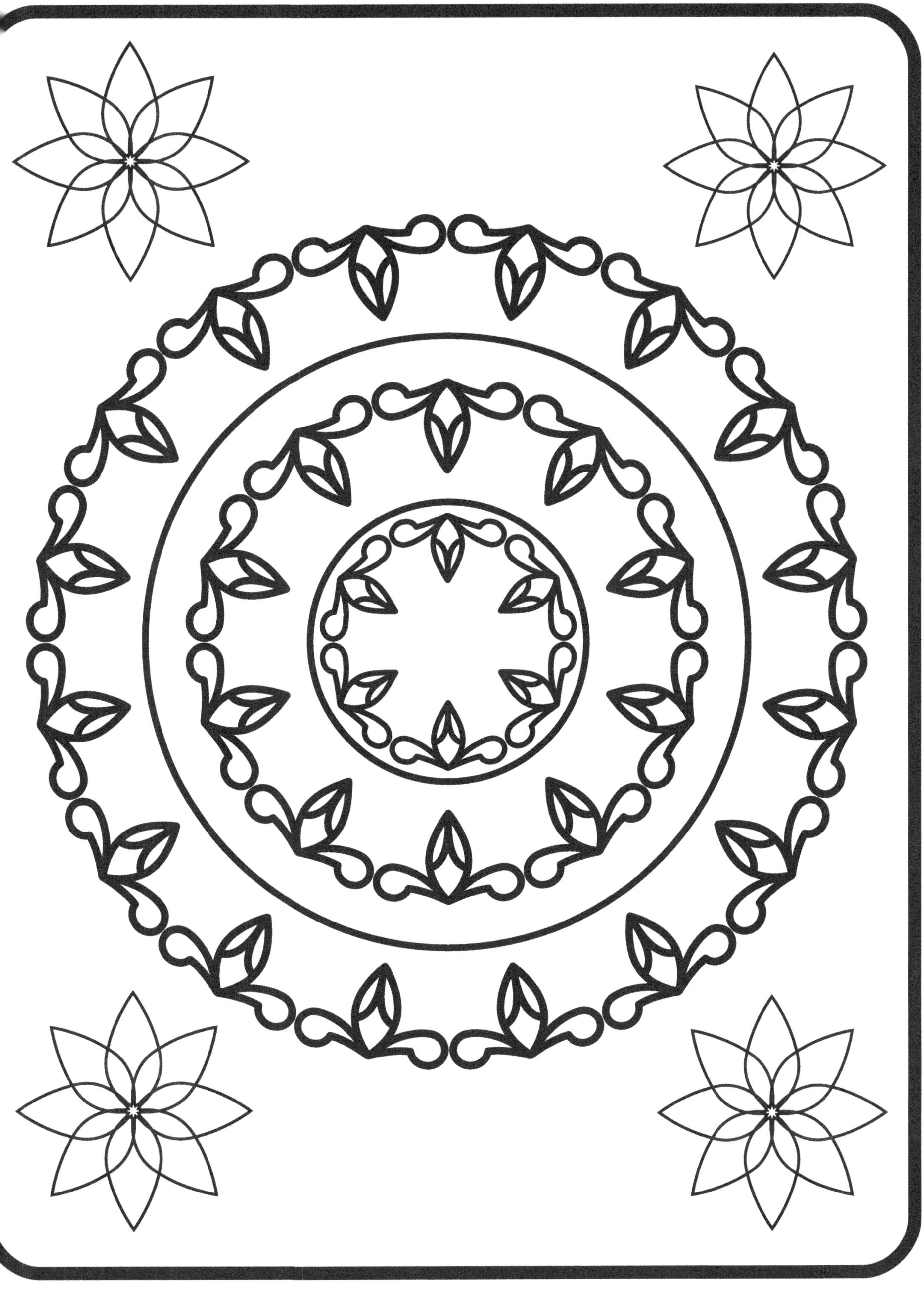

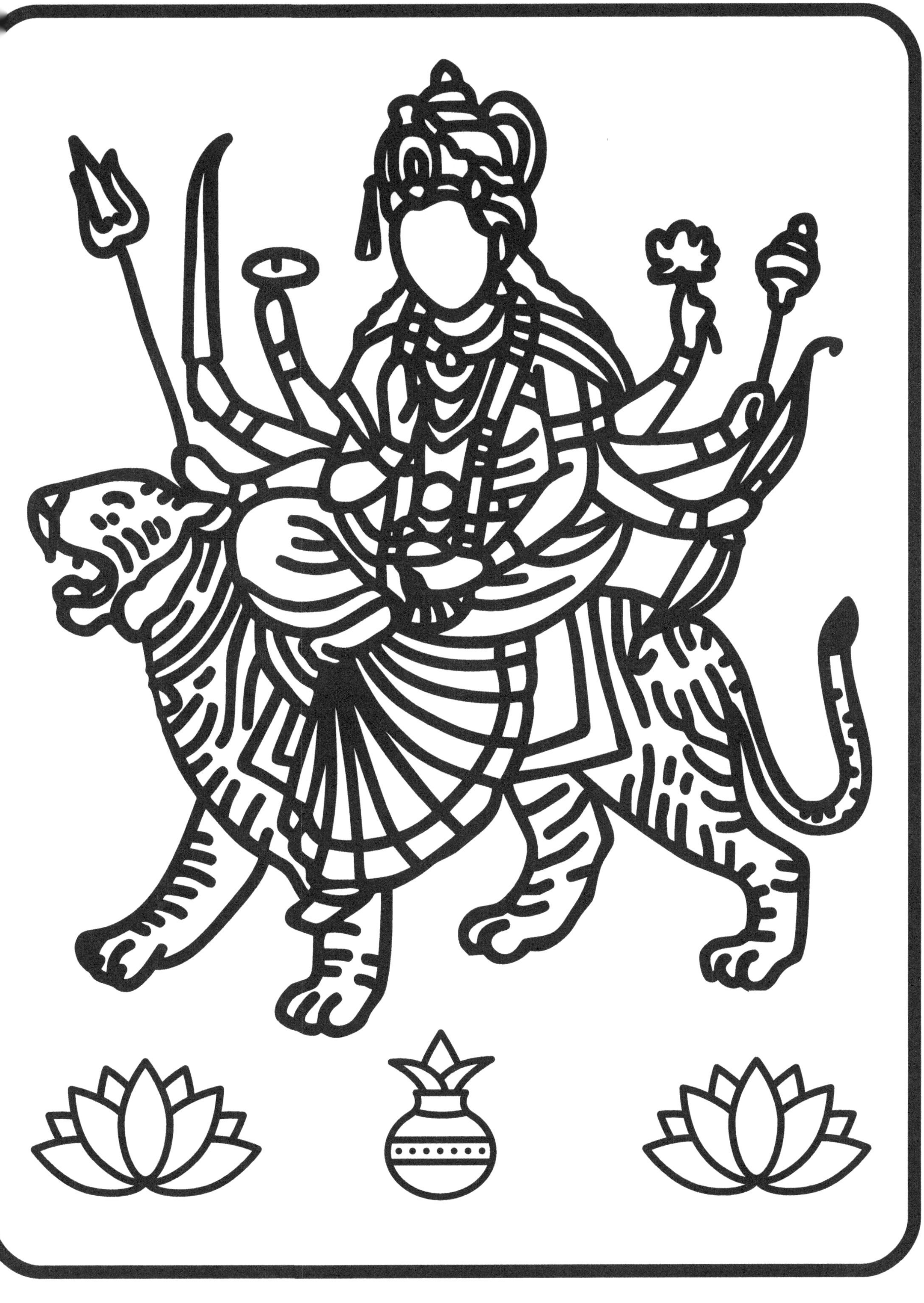

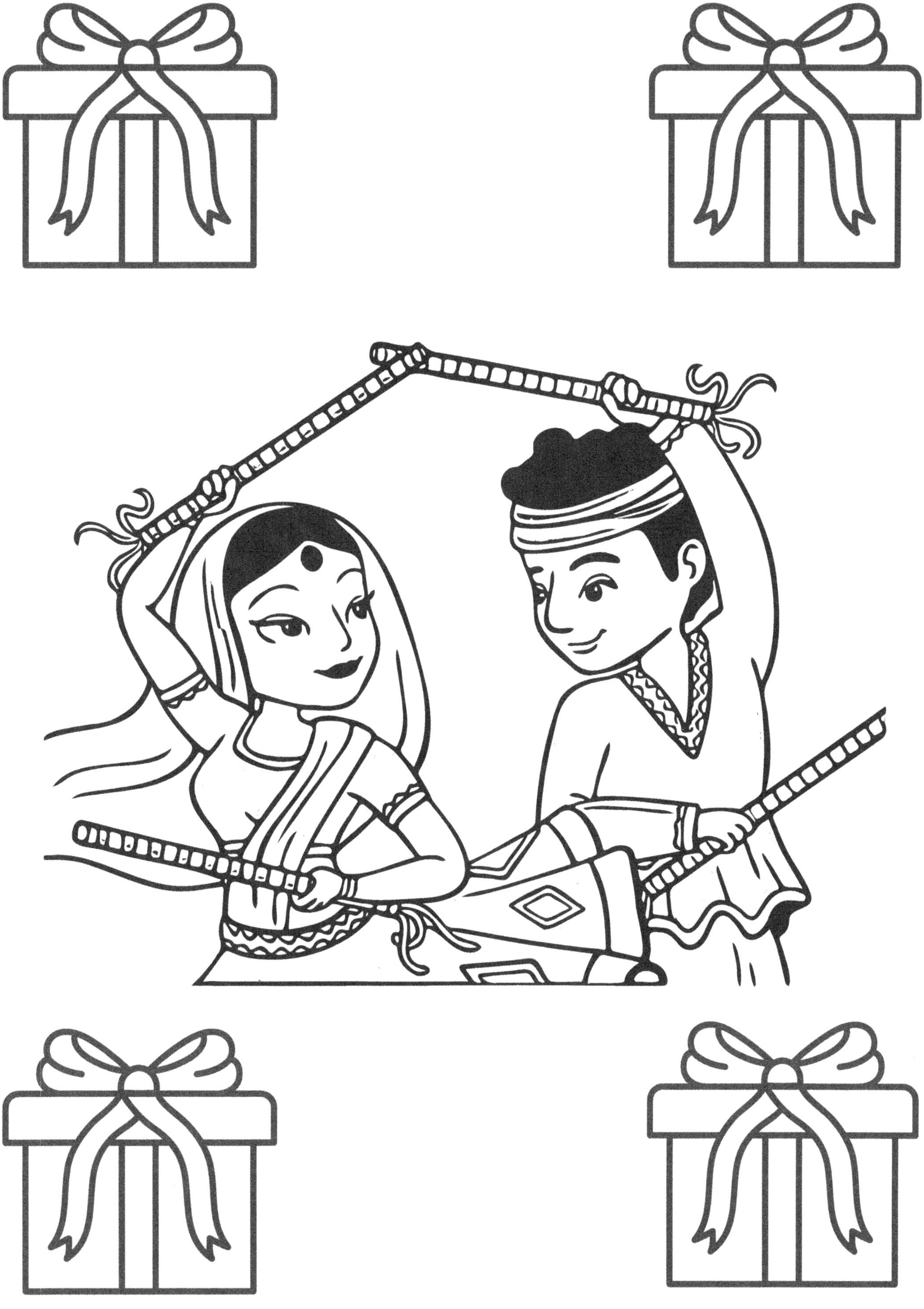

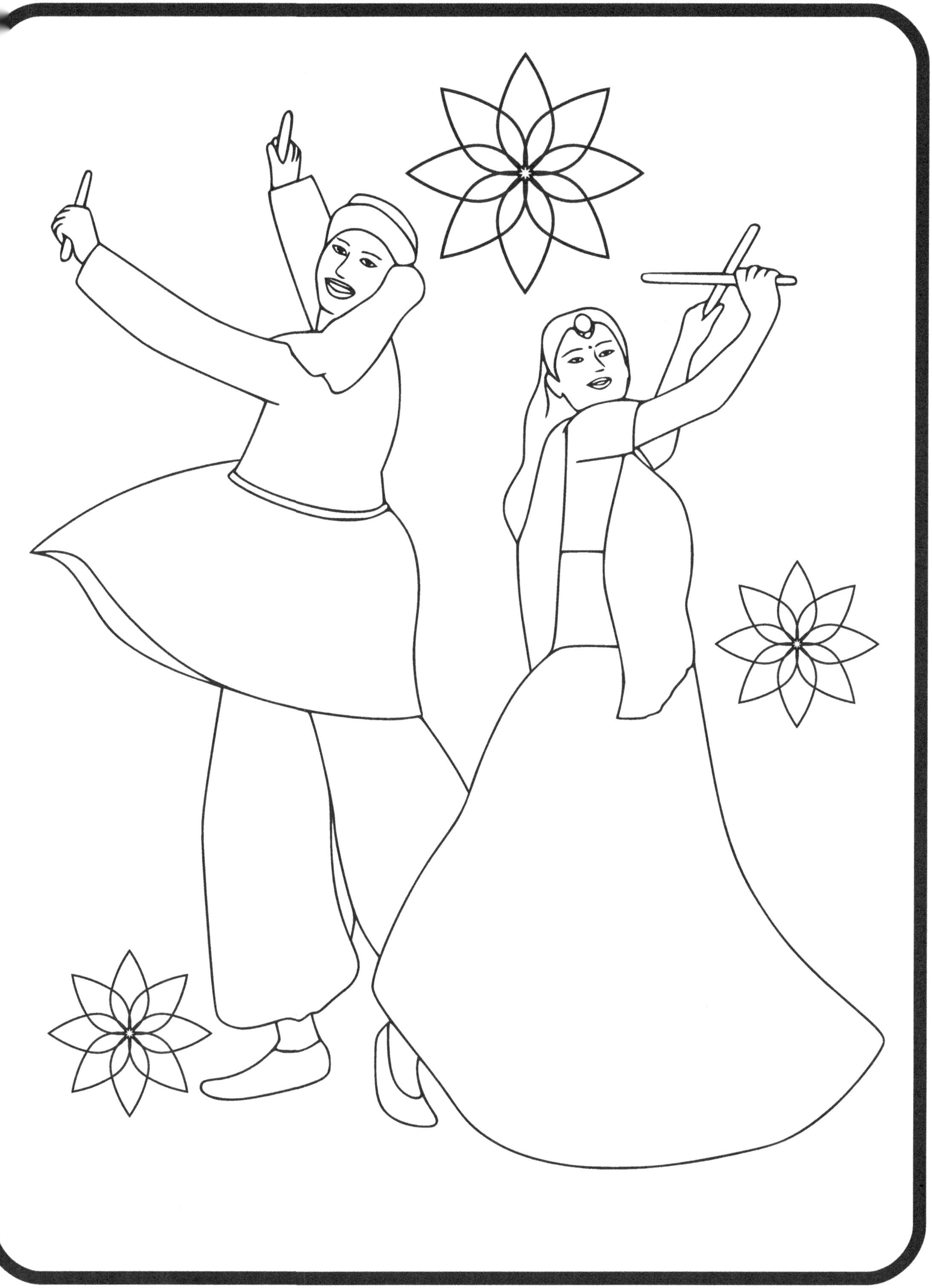

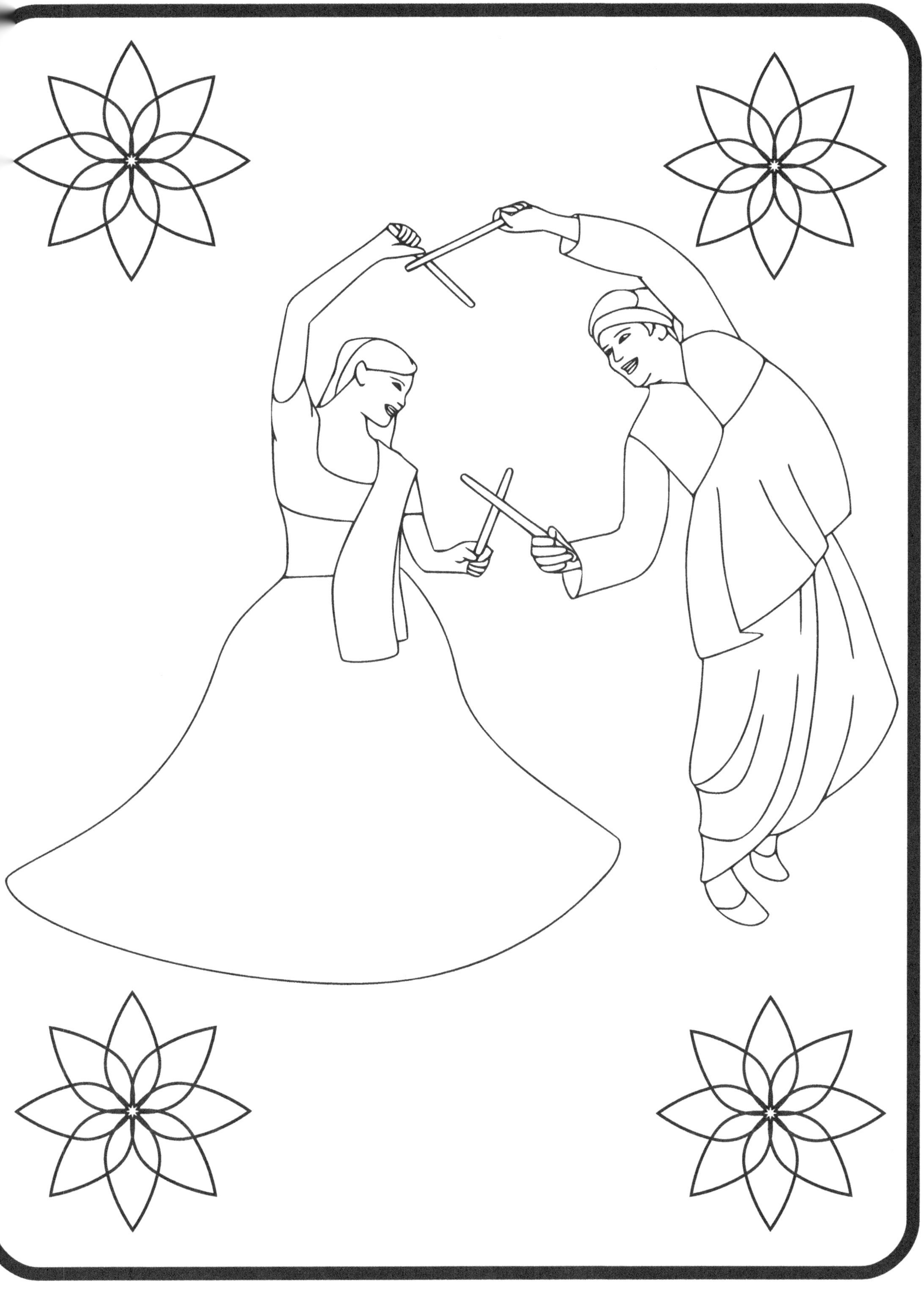

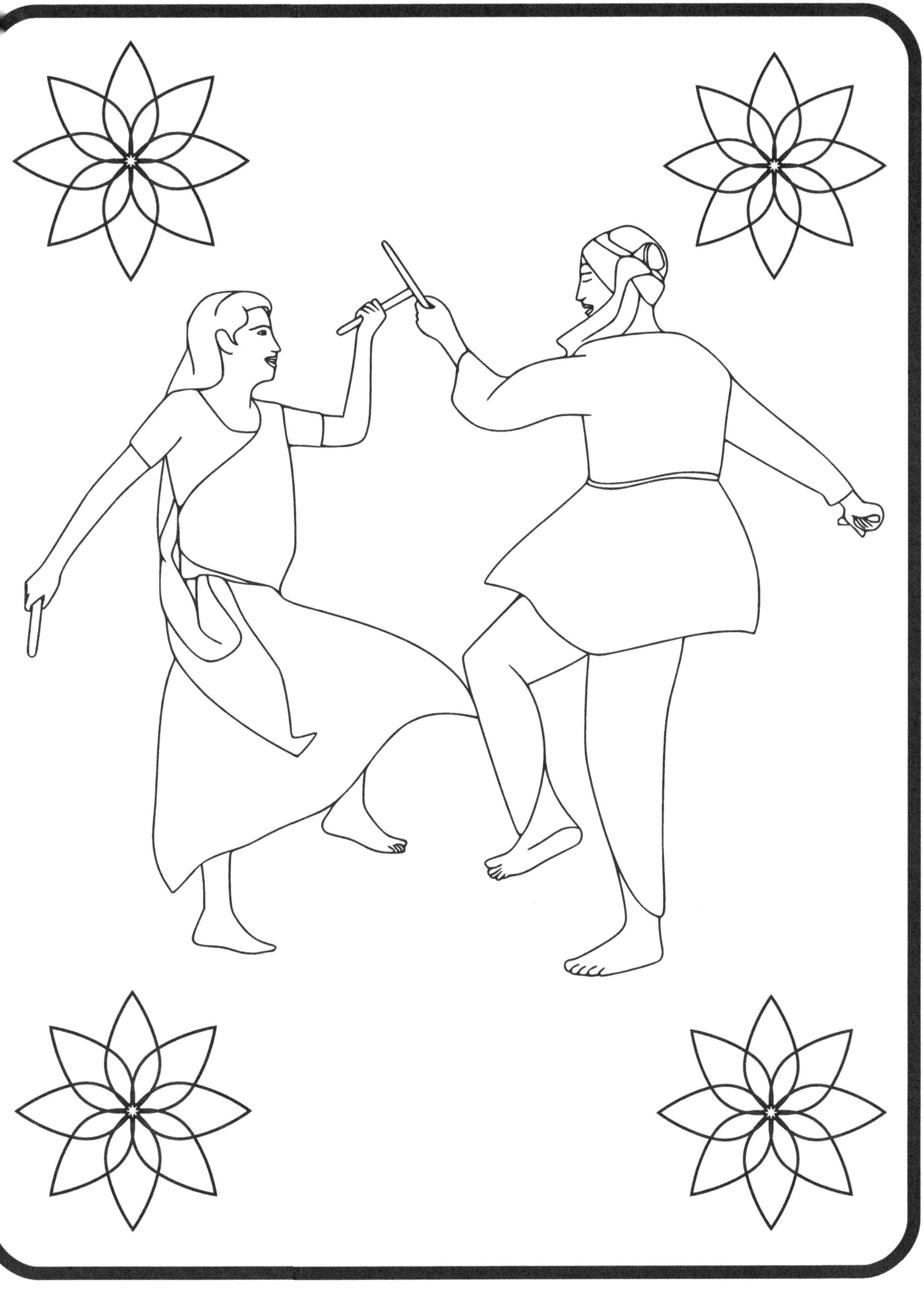

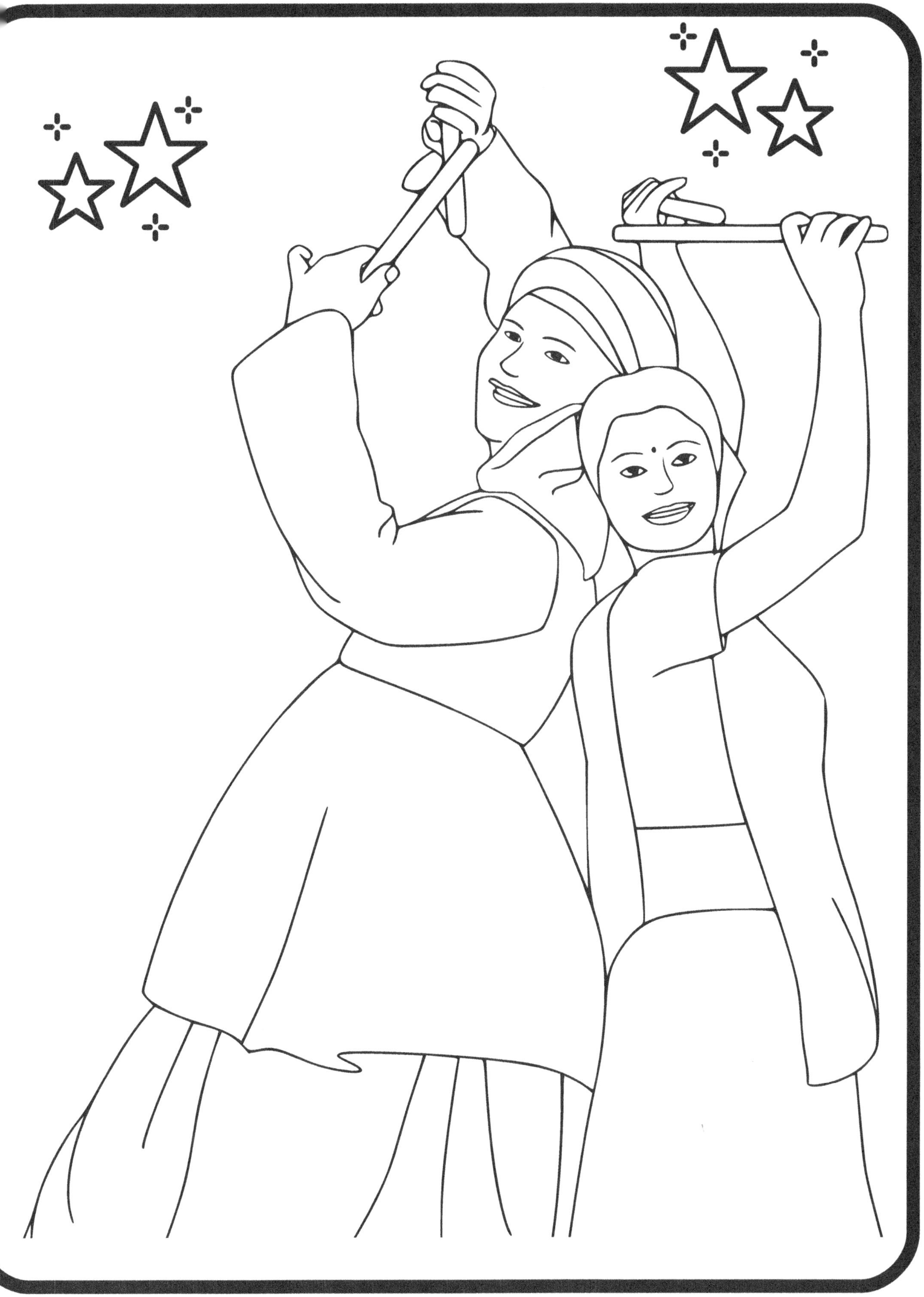

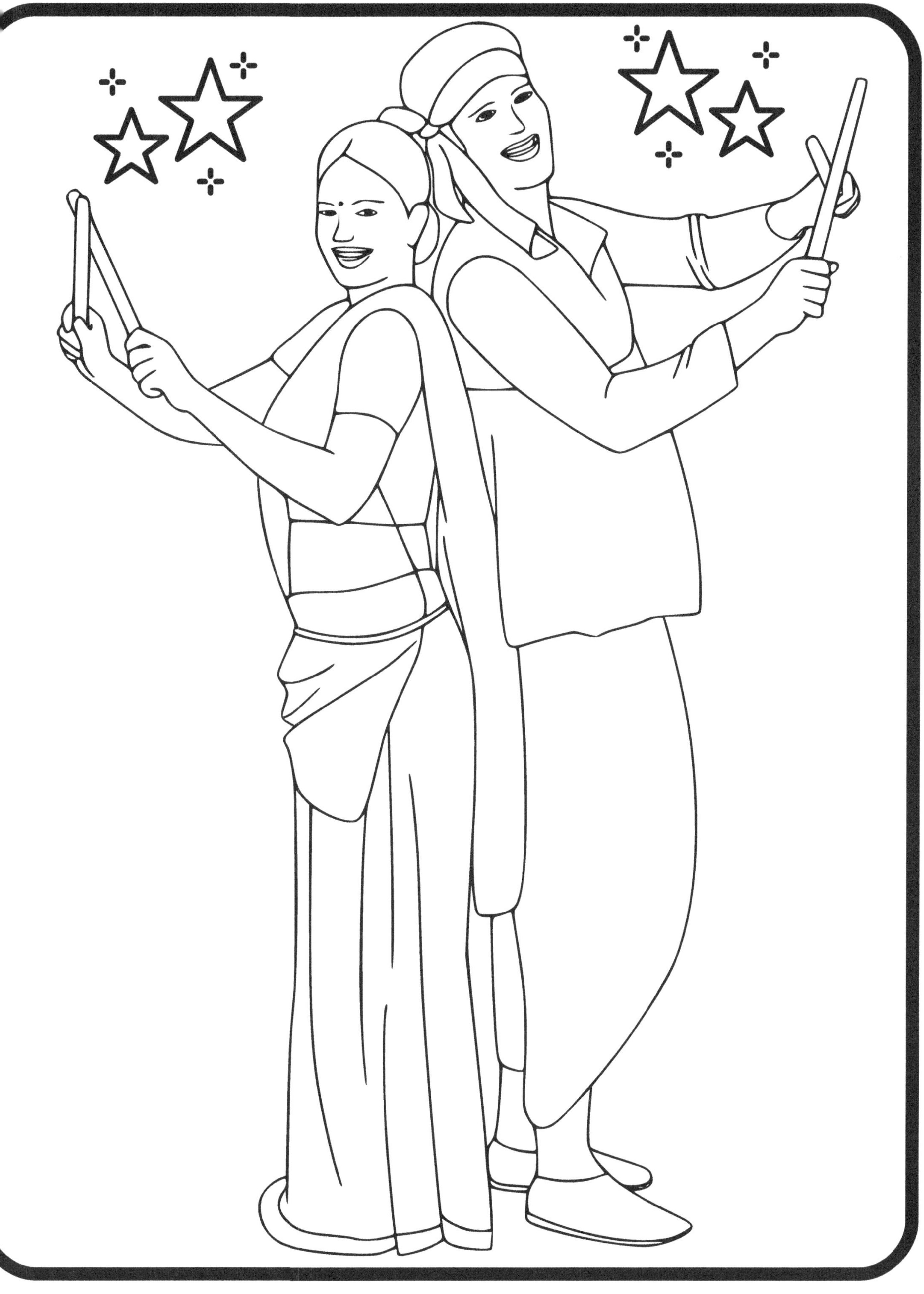

Made in the USA
Coppell, TX
07 October 2024

38253019R10024